Neuroscience of Mind Empowerment

Epigenetics, Neuroplasticity, Meditation, and Music Therapy

Anees Akhtar & Nasim Khan

authorHOUSE®

AuthorHouse™ UK
1663 Liberty Drive
Bloomington, IN 47403 USA
www.authorhouse.co.uk
Phone: 0800.197.4150

© 2017 Anees Akhtar & Nasim Khan. All rights reserved.

Contributing author: Muhammad Nasim Khan, PhD, PostDoc.

No part of this book may be reproduced, stored in a retrieval system, or transmitted by any means without the written permission of the author.

Published by AuthorHouse 06/02/2017

ISBN: 978-1-5246-7689-6 (sc)
ISBN: 978-1-5246-7690-2 (hc)
ISBN: 978-1-5246-7699-5 (e)

Print information available on the last page.

Any people depicted in stock imagery provided by Thinkstock are models, and such images are being used for illustrative purposes only.
Certain stock imagery © Thinkstock.

This book is printed on acid-free paper.

Because of the dynamic nature of the Internet, any web addresses or links contained in this book may have changed since publication and may no longer be valid. The views expressed in this work are solely those of the author and do not necessarily reflect the views of the publisher, and the publisher hereby disclaims any responsibility for them.

Dedicated to our late parents and sister

Anees extends heartfelt thanks to his supportive and loving wife

Contents

Acknowledgements ix
Introduction xi
Mission xiii

Chapter 1
Parapsychology, 'Sixth Sense', Love and Empathy 1

Chapter 2
How we Feel and Read other People's Thoughts and Feelings 7

Chapter 3
Chemical/Electromagnetic Nature of the Human Mind and Body 15

Chapter 4
Knowledge Enhances our Emotional Intelligence and Outlook 19

Chapter 5
Achieve your Goal and Reach your Destiny 25

Chapter 6
Epigenetics: How Thoughts can Alter your Genetic Makeup 31

Chapter 7
Neuroplasticity: Rewire and Alter the Structure of your Brain 41

Chapter 8
Music Therapies: Improve Neurodegenerative Diseases 55

Chapter 9
Meditation & Mindfulness: Combat Neurodegenerative Diseases 65

Glossary 75
References 97
Research papers reviewed 99
Anees Akhtar 101
Muhammad Nasim Khan 103

Acknowledgements

The development of this book has been a most stimulating journey and a learning experience for the authors.

We would like to express our affectionate gratitude to our brothers and sister for their support in completing this manuscript.

We are deeply grateful to M.A.A. Khan (late) for his consistent encouragement and keen interest in the development of our lifelong learning, research, writing, and speaking skills.

We are also indebted to the following friends and colleagues who have shown much interest and encouragement in the production of this book:

Professor Dr. Sarfraz Khan, Prof. Naseer Khan, and Dr. Faisal, for providing us opportunities to host seminars and workshops in their faculties and departments to enable us to share our knowledge with their academic staff and research students.

Professors Imtiaz and Khalid, Imtiaz Ali and Aziz Ali, deserve acknowledgement as well. We also extend our gratitude to Dr. Avais Chaudhary, Shafeeq-u-Zaman, Sarfraz Subedar, Arif Meo, Dr. Shareef-u-Zaman, and Dr. Azhar.

Special thanks are extended to Dr. Alan Hargreaves, Dr. Adrian Slater, Prof. Richard Jenkins, Dr. Mark Fowler, Dr. Sandra Kirk, Dr. Shamim Ahmad, Prof. Stephen Forsythe, and Dr. David Hughes, who have equipped our minds with scientific ideas and innovations in Psychology and Biomedical sciences.

We are grateful to Nottingham Speaker's Club (England) president, Alan Young, ex-president Martin Cox, Sandra Hart, and Dennis Apple, in extending to us opportunities to speak in club meetings.

Also appreciated are Jimmy Stuart and Scott Warren for extending invitations to talk in the Nottingham Philosophy Club (England) meetings.

We extend our thanks to CopyTight Associates for their transcribing, editing, and proofreading.

Lastly, but not least, our grateful thanks go to all the staff of AuthorHouse Publishing; and especially consultants Emmanuelle Daan, Andy Iverson, and Sydney Filicio.

Introduction

The Mind is the most powerful thing in the Universe. Mind Empowerment Science is the powerful methodology that enables us to harness all aspects of knowledge and wisdom to achieve success, health, wealth, and happiness, from the Universe. We can harness the mental ability of history's greatest thinkers, artists, and scientists, to allow their influence to expand our minds and create universal beauty and goodness in the world. For instance:

Philosophy: Aristotle, Frederick Engels, Georg Hegel. Karl Marx and Plato.

Science: Marie Curie, Thomas Edison, Albert Einstein, Galileo Galilei, Isaac Newton, Louis Pasteur, and Orville and Wilbur Wright.

Art: Michelangelo, Raphael, Rembrandt, and Leonardo da Vinci.

Literature: Charles Dickens, Faiz Ahmed Faiz, Victor Hugo, Allama Iqbal, Habib Jalib, John Keats, John Milton, William Shakespeare, and Percy Bysshe Shelley.

Psychology: Sigmund Freud, William James, Karl Jung, and Jean Piaget.

Music: Ludwig van Beethoven, Frederic Chopin, Wolfgang Amadeus Mozart, and Richard Wagner.

Mission

Our aim is to increase development of the abilities of the global population through the principles of 'Mind Potential Science', and its applications as a philosophy of leadership, self-motivation, individual achievement, and societal development.

Our purpose is to enlighten, through the fields of Neuropsychology and Success Philosophy, to empower the disadvantaged and people suffering from neurodegenerative diseases, and encourage all peoples' knowledge of the psychology and mechanics of achieving health, wealth, and happiness, and to develop understanding of the purpose of human beings in the Universe.

It is not our intention to dissuade anyone from his/her existing political, religious, economical schools of thought, or their professional fields.

This book's teachings focus on combatting negative thoughts, desires and impulses, and the toxic effects of unnecessary pharmaceutical drugs, etc., from all societies; the effects of which are toxifying the minds and bodies of people, and are preventing them from appreciating Nature, and Life's Potential.

We are committed to promoting the awareness of good mental and physical health of individuals in all societies.

We do not favour those who waste mental and physical energies through vengefulness, gossip, envy, selfishness, and negative competitive behaviour.

Instead, we encourage people to be philanthropically creative, focusing thoughts and actions on conquering our nature and fully experiencing the Universe.

Professional fields

We will only invoke creativity and boost mental power by teaching the use of the creative energy present in the universe to make the mind a powerful 'mind magnet'; necessary for harnessing creativity from the universe in the form of wisdom, health, wealth, and happiness. This ability can be cultivated; the more it is used, the more you will rely on it, and the more it will develop.

In spite of the clear benefits, the faculty of creative imagination is one that the majority of people never use;

and only a small number of people use with deliberation and purpose. Those who use this faculty actively and voluntarily, and understand its functions, are 'geniuses'. By observing the rules of mental discipline today, we will see the great leaders, scientists, artists, actors, athletes and creators of tomorrow.

Try to imagine the value and importance of this book's teachings and its potential to increase knowledge and enable achievement in all aspects of life. This knowledge includes the training of individuals associated with educational institutions from senior, through to general members of academic staff, who can apply this practical philosophy to themselves, their students and amongst wider society, enabling all to change their lives for the better.

By following the references and guidance given in this volume you will be able to empower your mind and understand how to develop your 'mind magnet' to harness the innovative ideas of your acquired knowledge; and use this to develop abilities ranging from high intelligence, to the skills needed to achieve your wishes of better health, wealth and happiness.

As authors, we feel it our responsibility to provide people with proven techniques and tools for personal growth; we have used all of the methods presented in this book personally in our lives – they helped shape our lives, as well as others.

To conclude, this book reflects the views and joint opinions of the co-authors.

Chapter 1

Parapsychology, 'Sixth Sense', Love and Empathy

"Happiness does not rise with standards of living, but only with the standards of loving."

The brain is not hard-wired from birth in the same way as a computer; the brain has the ability to change itself in response to things that happen in our environment. The theory of Epigenetics supports this idea and explains how the environment has profound effects on the expression of genes in their relative environments. Thoughts can change the structure and function of our brain, as well as the expression of genes.

By applying this knowledge and training to our brain, we can achieve life's aspirations and help defeat cancer, dementia, eating disorders, and other health issues, as well as develop a general sense of wellbeing.

The idea of Neuroplasticity is that our minds are designed to improve as we get older. The brain can be re-wired in a useful way that had previously been thought to be impossible – our thoughts and emotions can physically change our brain chemistry and function. Neuroplasticity can be a kind of 'superpower' in which success and happiness can be acquired just by re-programming our brain.

Deepak Chopra writes on the Chopra Centre website: "Regardless of the nature of the genes we inherit from our parents, dynamic change in our thoughts has unlimited influence in our fate".

The following activities can physically increase our brain strength, size, and density:

- Applying stimulants of creativity to artificially activate dopamine and endorphins for creative purposes.
- Consuming foods such as blueberries, dark chocolate and green tea.
- Practising yoga, meditation, playing the piano, and puzzle games like Sudoku.

'Sixth Sense' provokes our Creative Imaginative Faculty of Mind.

"Imaginations are more important than knowledge"

Creativity is the flashes of thoughts in our 'imaginative creative faculty of mind' which are produced in the form of 'hunches' in our conscious mind, utilizing brainstorming and mindfulness, by for instance, being alone, or sitting in a dark room. The 'sixth sense' creates these flashes in our mind; although scientists have not yet been able to locate them, they can confirm that they definitely have a function in our mind.

To access and use your 'sixth sense', you must activate and train your mind to accept these flashes; we must not ignore them, but utilize and enjoy them, and write about them. When they occur, 'infinite intelligence' is activated – our minds are able to purify thoughts and provide solutions to intellectual, business, and spiritual issues.

Throughout history scientists, writers, creators, and thinkers have used their 'sixth sense' effectively and accessed these flashes of thought and inspiration to achieve innovations and patency in research and development – all by using the 'sixth sense' and harnessing the treasures of wisdom and creation from the Universe.

You can follow the different stimulants of creativity; exercising, achieving fame, developing friendship for intellectual purposes, playing games, appreciating food and music and playing a musical instrument – all have the natural ability to produce endorphins and dopamine – the neurotransmitters of wisdom and creativity.

The knowledge that you'll acquire by engaging in the above, and activating the "creative faculty of your mind", is the most reliable of all forms of knowledge.

The American, Dr. Elmer R. Gates, completed 200 patents in which his imagination was stimulated by sitting in a darkened room and waiting for such mental flashes to occur; he earned his living by 'sitting for ideas' for some of America's largest corporations.

Love and Empathy Flourish in our Brain Regions

Effects of positive thinking, love, and empathy on the following areas of the brain:

1. Limbic brain

Humans, and lower animal species, are born with a limbic brain. It is linked with empathy, love, affection, and emotions of nurturing and training their offspring with lifelong skills. Reptiles do not have this specialized brain area, and therefore can kill and eat their young, and may not always differentiate their young from prey; notwithstanding, for instance, the protective behaviour seen in crocodiles. The presence of the limbic brain in other animals and humans has created empathy and nurturing behaviour toward their coming generations.

2. Vagus Nerves:

The two vagus nerves are the longest of the cranial nerves and are sometimes referred to as the "wandering nerves". Extending from the brainstem and branching out to multiple organs, including the oesophagus, heart, lungs, and digestive system, they form part of the (involuntary) *autonomic nervous system* that commands unconscious body functions. They also have a role in regulating the immune system. Charles Darwin called sympathy the strongest of all human instincts.

If you are witness to suffering, or are presented with an image of suffering you will most likely react with compassion; your heart rate will most likely decrease, and you may be impelled to comfort and support the sufferer. If you experience these feelings and physical reactions it's because humans are 'hard-wired' for it.

An empathetic response such as this is 'activated' by the vagus nerves.

3. Sociopathy

Sociopathy is a psychological condition in which the part of the brain responsible for our empathetic attitudes is damaged, resulting in persons who cannot maintain normal positive social behaviours. They function on a superficial level, however, appearing and behaving 'normally'.

A similar behavioural condition occurs in sociopathy caused by a brain-damaging incident such as a stroke or accident trauma.

Similarly, when we abuse our power and start ignoring other people's feelings and opinions, we radiate an arrogant, ignorant behaviour, and it becomes the default nature of our thinking.

Alternatively, empathy, humbleness, and care-giving behaviours provide us with more authentic, dependable, power and trust in society.

4. Love follows spiritual laws

Love is not a game – you should know the odds. Love is spiritual. Nobody wants fake love – all people want real love. For real love you have to learn its spiritual and ethical laws. That is why in human history spiritual and ethical laws have been the foundation of all great collaborations and romances. When adhering to spiritual and ethical laws your intuitive heart and neuroplastic brain become expanded; your relationships are strengthened by spiritual love.

Chapter 2

How we Feel and Read other People's Thoughts and Feelings

<u>Charles Darwin – Ideas of thought and feeling:</u>

The Universe is made up of thoughts which are combined to make 'infinite intelligence'. According to certain schools of thought there is a "cosmic mind" formed by the universe that has the ability to restore, proliferate, perceive, and bring forth thoughts to mind according to mental activity. You can switch on and off the frequency of thoughts by just changing what you think and feel; such as creating a feeling of peacefulness and relaxation by listening to soothing music, by meditation, engaging in creative discussion, or by exercising to feel more invigorated.

Joanna Crosse in her book, "Find Your Voice", cited the experiment of the Japanese scientist, Dr. Masaru Emoto, who explained that "words have power in themselves". His research suggested that molecules of water are affected by our thoughts, words, and feelings. As water makes up to 70% of our body, bad words negatively affect the structure of water, whereas good words help – as in Dr. Emoto's snowflake crystals, taking beautiful shapes when exposed to words of love and gratitude – then by inference creating 'beautiful' water molecules.

According to Dr. Emoto, words are an expression of the soul and the condition of our soul has a large impact on water. The language we use and the words we choose are vitally important, and verbal insult can have dangerous and damaging psychological effects – Joanna Crosse writes, "words and language have tremendous power, as does the intent behind them".

The tone of the voice also has the ability to heal. Certain voices can keep your attention whereas others don't. When we listen to a wonderful rich resonant voice, it can feel very therapeutic. If someone says something loving and kind to you in a gentle tone of voice it's likely to make you feel good – but if someone yells at you in a harsh way then it's going to have a destructive effect.

The words we say originate from our thoughts. Thoughts can be toxic or good, depending on the way you behave and how you think and feel; so try to avoid toxic thoughts – they are more harmful than an unhealthy diet. Our hijacked amygdala is not always prone to sustain good thoughts because in the history of evolution, negative emotions, like fear and anger, have great *survival* value, which impel a threatened animal to fight or flight.

According to Charles Darwin our ability to send and read emotions has played an enormous role in human evolution, both in creating and maintaining social order, particularly with negative feelings; we usually respond more strongly to someone who is angry than to someone who is in a good mood, creating a loop of negativity or rage.

How did we become spiritual survival machines on this planet?

Our chemical and electromagnetic nature has made us a spiritual survival machine on this planet, and a subtotal of the subatomic manifestation of the bi-symmetrical nature of the universe. Our brain is a powerful 'receiving and transmission tower'; our feet and toes, hands and fingers, are like sensors that detect signals from the Earth and Universe, passing them via the nervous system to the brain, broadcasting feelings and thoughts through the brain that are detected from the environment. The two symmetries of the bi-symmetrical universe is analogous with the way the brain's left and right hemispheres are joined by the white & grey matter; by chemical bonding the junction between the two hemispheres connects the two halves of the brain by the neural connections. We have 86 billion neurons in both halves of the brain, and each neuron can connect with other neurons; there are from 5000 to 10000 different connections.

The number of neurons in the human brain is more than all the stars of the universe and is the basic information processing unit that is responsible for understanding, memories, and our behaviour. Interconnected neurons make up the structure of the brain. As the signals are passed on, the neurons create a network by firing and wiring between these neurons, creating our personalities and helping us to perceive the world around us.

When we try to remember the name of a person or recollect what we read in a book, a neural network will develop a memory of this through neurotransmitters that build the chemical and electrical signals to bridge the gap between two neurons.

The Human brain:

- Is the most complex and mysterious machine in the Universe.
- Its power is many-fold higher than a basic modern computer.
- Its storage capacity is about 1000 terabytes.
- It does millions of different things at once.
- It stores the day's events at night, and can catalogue, archive and recall memories at a later date.
- You cannot hear, feel, or think about it – the brain mostly acts subconsciously; but the more you actively exercise your brain the more it will benefit you.

- It is the organ that controls and operates the body's neural systems, made up of around 80 billion to 100 billion nerve cells (neurons).

The brain is used to:

- Store memories
- Control our body functions
- Communicate and react to our surroundings.
- Give us power to think.

Neurochemistry:

The Human brain has the following composition:
- 78% water
- 10% lipids
- 8% proteins
- 1% carbohydrates
- 2% solid organics
- 1% inorganic salts

Amygdala:

Socially active people have the largest amygdala; the part of brain that plays a big role in social and mental wellbeing – therefore it is important to build more grey matter in the brain by understanding more about the world around us.

Earth's first life-forms were prokaryotes. Several billion years later human beings have evolved to become complex multi-cellular forms. We evolved into advanced homo-sapiens forms by developing, adapting and controlling our minds and bodies. Two hundred thousand years ago when humans learned to command fire, they started cooking the meat of hunted animals which led to less energy required for digestion. Consequently this led to increased blood supply to the brain instead of the stomach. This excess blood in our brain has allowed it to adapt and to grow in size and functionality, therefore increasing the speed and nature of our thoughts. It is by this evolution that the human race became the dominant species on this planet.

Over the past few centuries our intelligence has sharpened with the advancement of technology and medicine. The brain is split into two parts:

Left hemisphere.
Right hemisphere.

Left side of the brain controls:

- Speech
- Writing
- Logics

Right side of the brain controls:

- Creativity
- Emotions
- Information

Information is processed as quickly as 120 meters / second, or 268 miles per hour, in the brain. The weight of the human brain is about 1.4kg. It is relatively bigger than that of almost any other animal. The human mind is the most powerful 'receiving and transmission tower' in the Universe. Around 60,000 thoughts per day are perceived and proliferated by it – by knowing our feelings we can control our thoughts.

Humans are curious about the world around them. They not only accumulate extra food, like lower animals, but they want to know what lies over the horizon for the pure joy of it.

Even though people may not be great thinkers, they can understand the concepts of truth, justice, or honesty.

Creativity is a fundamental part of our nature and human beings are in constant search for new ways to do things; and for new things to do.

Societies devoting a huge amount of energy on science, art and literature advance further than those that ignore these endeavours – as creativity breeds more creativity we should make a habit of creative thinking.

CHAPTER 3

Chemical/Electromagnetic Nature of the Human Mind and Body

<u>Newton's law of attraction and prevailing love in nature and the Universe:</u>

All chemical and electromagnetic processes of the human body and brain function similarly to all electrical and magnetic entities and bodies in the universe; from atom to solar system, galaxies and all life on this planet – all are linked to each other through chemical and electromagnetic attraction and communication.

Similarly, as in the human body, plant and animal 'cell signalling mechanisms', and chemical communication between microbes in the form of 'Quorum sensing', is the greatest manifestation of the law of attraction and love in Nature and the Universe; the same law co-ordinates the galaxies, solar systems, and life on our beautiful planet. This is the law of attraction, or love in nature; or Newton's 2nd Law of Gravity.

Scattered matter in the Universe

After the 'Big Bang', matter has been scattered throughout the universe, and is present in living and non-living things to the point that it is difficult to understand fully its mechanism of action on living and non-living things. In some situations it is partially explained and understood at its atomic and molecular level, but still a lot of work has to be done in physics, chemistry, and biology to fully understand its mysterious mechanism of action.

New branches of these sciences, like genetic engineering and nanotechnologies, will use a lot of its theoretical and practical approaches to make new innovations in coming decades – which will open up some new debates among researchers – to fully understand the mechanisms of action in living and non-living things.

Still, the issues of protein-folding and the mechanisms of division of the AIDS' virus proteins – and artificial and therapeutic repairs of damaged DNA – may remain a mystery for the foreseeable future.

We have not yet harnessed the full form of chemical energy, as produced in chemical forms in plants, insects, microbes and animal and human tissues, in the form of alkaloids, steroids, proteins, hormones, antibodies and antibiotics.

Should we be able to harness all chemical forms of energy, from the above sources in the future – we would be able to find the cure of Cancer, AIDS, Hepatitis, Arthritis, and various cardiovascular diseases, and for many genetic disorders to which certain people are predisposed.

Quantum Physics and Consciousness

Human consciousness has not yet fully understood the dynamic functions of the different energy forms in the universe, which is in the form of energy beams of 'infinite intelligence'.

This form of energy may be in the form of photons, quarks, waves, or as a chemical or electromagnetic form. This energy sometimes combines chemically and electromagnetically to form proteins, hormones, antibodies, antibiotics and vaccines.

When human consciousness fully understands the different forms of energy, and can harness their dynamic uses, the human mind, culture, societies and health conditions will advance greatly through the adaptation of new technologies, new ways of thinking and beliefs in science, art, culture, and philosophy. When 'infinite intelligence' and human consciousness becomes harmonized, it harnesses its form and enables the creation of new innovations. Many inventions and creations come into existence when we are intensely focused on thoughts, utilizing the 'sixth sense' to boost our creative imaginative faculty. We are medically, technologically and culturally conscious or hyperconscious, in as much as we know about the different energy forms responsible for dynamically activating in the universe. Harnessing this energy, either in atomic, molecular or chemical form, gives us consciousness and improves humans medically, technologically and culturally, enabling us to empower our minds and experience a new consciousness of thought, hidden in the folded energy beams in the universe.

CHAPTER 4

Knowledge Enhances our Emotional Intelligence and Outlook

<u>Emotional intelligence and the value of acquiring and promoting knowledge:</u>

"Dig deeper into the emotional reservoir."

Psychologists have proven that people who had *actively* tried to improve their personalities got more jobs as executives than those who had inferior personalities but greater abilities – it is said in China, 'man who cannot smile must not open the shop.'

A smile is magnetic and a frown is un-magnetic (not attractive); it takes more facial muscles to frown than it does to smile.

Optimistic vs pessimistic:

People who are optimistic, bright, and hopeful are more popular and attractive to others – people want to be around them. Pessimists constantly bemoan their losses in life; always dwelling on the bad things that have happened to them, or that they expect to happen.

Be optimistic rather than pessimistic and avoid talking about sickness, accidents, failure, and unhappiness – instead talk about pleasure and happy events.

Reasons to be an optimist:

- Optimists live longer than pessimists and have a 50% lower risk of an early death than pessimists.
- Optimists have fewer physical and emotional or health problems – they suffer less pain and they have increased energy and generally feel more peaceful, happier and calmer than pessimists – being an optimism protects you from illness.

Positive attitude is so important because it boosts our immune systems, enabling us to fight illness. Positive people were found to be more resistant to the influenza virus than negative people when exposed to an infectious environment. Research studies into positive attitudes have revealed positivity to be the best prevention against heart diseases.

According to Dr. David Hamilton, people who are most satisfied with their lives live longer because satisfaction in life means taking interest in life and the means of happiness

Complaining is a contagious behaviour

Complaining about things and people affects those around us. When we complain around people we trigger their dominant complaining instinct. They are also likely to find fault with life and the world in general; it is contagious behaviour which affects the people around us.

Our keen observations and research shows that when we have a certain goal, and imagine our destiny, our minds focus on that goal and achieving targets associated with that destiny, but as soon as we get bored and lose sight of our destiny we suddenly view life more negatively and start complaining about trivial matters, or opposing things, and may become disillusioned with life.

One thing that can boost your morale is to share your power, wealth, happiness, and status, with other people. It's possible to achieve more happiness by giving away money to people and charities; by showing this generosity (even if it's a small amount of your salary) you share your strength, knowledge, happiness and other attributes and experience a boost in your morale and a feelings of contentment. Similarly, our positive attitude toward our aging mind and body reduces the incidence of high blood pressure (hypertension) and heart diseases. By visualizing the happier moments of our younger life we can reduce the physiological and anatomical aging process, which will enable us to feel sharper, look younger, and feel more energized. The sense of gratitude and visualizing the positive effects of achieving a goal can help to boost your potential to do more, and achieve more; be courteous and kind when dealing with others and eventually you will reap the benefits of doing so….

Interior vs exterior of your personality:

Your outer personality is that which you show to the world. It is important this profile should present a true and honest, well clothed and groomed being, with a cheerful and happy countenance; displaying the qualities of a 'million dollar personality'.

If the interior side is coloured by thoughts of unhappiness, fear, failure, worry, hate, envy, and revenge, you will soon reflect this negative mental attitude to the outer world, and it will drive people away from you.

"What you habitually think, you will become."

The interior aspects of ourselves have had long-lasting effects on our personality – therefore dig deeper into the emotional reservoir and keep your thoughts beautiful and inspiring, and your outer personality will also be beautiful.

Build positive qualities like friendliness, trust, confidence, loyalty, cheerfulness, happiness, honesty, goodness, trustfulness, and clarity in your mind, and they will shine through and be obvious for all to see – there is a natural system of accountability, judgement, punishment, or reward in your Parasympathetic Nervous System:

"God will forgive your sins, but your nervous system won't."

Value of Acquiring and Promoting Knowledge.

The ability to learn, pass on knowledge, and to teach others, allows knowledge to be accumulated and thus a civilization can be created.
Civilization distinguishes the human species from all other forms of life. Every society needs to encourage and promote learning amongst its citizens or risk being left behind and eventually dominated by neighbouring societies. There is more awareness and consciousness in families, societies, and states where reading and study is common.

Speed-Reading promotes retention of knowledge

The basic techniques of speed reading were developed in the 1950s by the American educator, Evelyn Wood. She set up institutes for students to develop the ability to read hundreds of words per minute – many businessmen and politicians have studied her methods; U.S.A. Presidents, Jimmy Carter, and John F. Kennedy are regarded as famous speed-readers.

Chapter 5

Achieve your Goal and Reach your Destiny

Our lecture series output:

"Don't just make a living, make a life"

When we came to believe in ourselves we started writing and speaking to tell others about our feelings and experiences. Other people around us gained inspiration from our ideas, growing wisdom, and concepts.

Other people started to believe our view that we can use this knowledge and wisdom to strengthen faith in ourselves, other people, and *'Infinite Intelligence'*.

Our minds are capable of influencing our fate and wellbeing. Our audience started to apply the principles we taught them, and they found that these belief systems and faith in their subconscious mind can combat diseases and attain goals in their lives.

These elaborated techniques of visualization, affirmation, and autosuggestion, strengthen people's 'faith', and helps them to build a strong fabric of mind for positive thinking, enhancing their mind, body, and the world around them. This subsequently leads to demand for more explanation of the truth about the nature of the human mind, and to elicit more and more from the *'universal infinite intelligence'* in the form of health, wealth, prosperity, happiness, and strong relationships.

Most of the people to whom we have been presenting these concepts started believing that these are real principles. Consequently by applying these principles they started utilizing the maximum capacity of their minds; which for a normal person is usually not more than 5 - 10%, in their whole life.

These principles of mind empowerment science, epigenetics, neuroplasticity, mindfulness, and music therapy have the potential of maximizing mental capability and capacity, to take control of your whole body-complex systems in a more harmonious manner.

We can control our mind, which is the monitor of our body-systems, i.e. your digestive, respiratory, circulatory, nervous, and endocrine systems. Consequently our body systems are more harmonious and healthy, extending longevity by cultivating a positive mental attitude. You can combat illness and pain by instilling an optimistic approach toward the environment and by expanding your positive 'mind magnet', or neuroplastic nature of your mind.

By positive attitude, and by habit of gratitude, you can detoxify any relationship around you, can synchronize any heart, and get the benefit of new constructive reactions, due to this pleasurable feeling of inner balance.

Part two of lecture

The second principle and rule, that we applied on ourselves and taught others, to get the maximum achievement, is to utilize your subconscious mind, write down affirmations daily and follow them, and write down the short-term and long-term goals to be achieved in your path to a big destiny. The most important, and having highest impact on Man's health, wealth and happiness and abundance, is by brainstorming, meditation, and visualization, to set up your destiny or major goal in your life that will move your mind toward your goal, without any fear or hesitation.

If you have a properly written goal and destiny that you want to reach over the period of 1-3 years' time you will have a strong positive impact on your body immune system and your willpower. This action will reduce all negative emotions, like fear and procrastination, from the mind; your predominant thoughts will be goal-oriented and will alter your whole mental and genetic makeup.

You will start making new perceptions of the world around you. Then you will become the successful captain and commander of your life and fate.

You will soon feel that you have designed a ladder to climb to the 'beautiful palace' of your goals. Your subconscious mind and universal infinite intelligence and cosmic mind, or paranormal divine energy, has started autopilot work to achieve successes in your life.

This is how the universe is leveraged – the law of attraction starts working – and God, the 'universal infinite intelligence', starts blessings of wisdom, health, wealth, prosperity, and abundance on such a mind.

And you will feel a 'heaven on earth' by achieving this inner balance in the heart and mind. This is the way of the wise, noble, honest, and 'million-dollar mind'. You may have everything from prosperity, affluence, and abundance in life, but also have the blessings of bliss and tranquillity.

Consequently you have been successful in *shifting yourself* from a material survival machine to a spiritual being which has a higher purpose in life.

Purposeful life

The third principle, applied on ourselves, is to set up a mission in your life, because mission-orientated people are more resilient to adverse conditions in their life. They work hard to reach their goal and complete their mission which strengthens their immune system and extends their longevity of life.

By setting up these noble goals you set up a chain of constructive chemical reactions in your body and mind, and your subconscious will start surveillance of the conscious mind to fulfil these goals.

Only the mission-orientated life can teach you the higher purpose of human beings in the universe. This is the secret of finding the truth lying over the horizon of universal mysteries, which should be explored by the human mind. Hence you set up a written goal and destiny to reach; you give a purpose and meaning to your life, you live a purposeful life and automatically develop in yourself the habits of successful and million-dollar-minded people.

Your mission in life may be philanthropy, a mission of serving humanity with the ideas of loving, peace, prosperity, abundance, affluence, tranquillity, and bliss in every human life.

But if you have no such written and instructed navigator in your mind you will have to wander-lost, and chances are you will be deviated from the goal and destiny and you will be unsuccessful and lost in your life.

CHAPTER 6

Epigenetics: How Thoughts can Alter your Genetic Makeup

The new science of self-empowerment:

Epigenetics is a new revolutionary field in Biology. Epigenetics means control above genetics. It means that environmental influences, like nutrition, stress, and emotions can modify genes without changing their basic blueprint. These modifications of genes can be passed on to future generations, as the DNA blueprints are passed on via the double helix.

When DNA is uncovered, the cell makes the copy of the exposed gene which means that activity of the gene is controlled by the presence or absence of the covering proteins, which are controlled by environmental signals.

Epigenetic research predicts how environmental signals control the activity of genes. According to this research, the information goes to regulatory protein, to DNA, to RNA, resulting in protein synthesis.

Epigenetic research has shown that there are two mechanisms by which organisms pass on hereditary information. These mechanisms provide a way for scientists to study both the contribution of genes and control of epigenetics in human behaviour. If we only focus on DNA blueprints, then the influence of environment is impossible to understand.

Research shows that information that controls biology starts with environmental signals that in turn control the activity of regulatory proteins of DNA. Regulatory protein directs the activity of genes.

DNA, RNA, and protein functions are the same as described in the DNA model. As flow of information is no longer unidirectional, RNA could go against the predicted flow of information and can rewrite the DNA programme, which is called *reverse transcriptase*, a molecular mechanism by which RNA can re-write the genetic code; as reverse transcriptase or RNA is used by the AIDS virus to command the infected DNA cells.

It is known that epigenetic changes in the DNA molecule, such as adding or removing methyl chemical groups, can influence binding of regulatory proteins. Proteins are also responsible for the predicted flow of information, as protein antibodies in immune cells are involved with changing the DNA in the cells that synthesize them.

As environmental signals affect us epigenetically, regulatory proteins can 'dial up' and create 2000 or more variations of protein from the same blueprint.

Modification in genes by environmental signalling can pass from one generation to the next generation.

Bruce Lipton performed an experiment on mice that were predisposed to cardiovascular disease, diabetes, and cancer. The mice were fed with a methyl group-rich supplement. As methylation of DNA can silence or modify gene activity, and is involved with epigenetic modifications, consequently when methyl groups attach to gene DNA it changes the way the regulatory chromosomal protein binds to the DNA molecule. When protein binds tightly to the gene it can be removed by the environmental signals, so the gene can be read. This is why methylation of DNA is able to silence or modify gene activity; this chemical application subsequently prevented the mice developing the cancers.

The optimistic and pessimistic attitude 'taught' in childhood, and subsequently 'learned' in stressful environmental circumstances, also affects telomerase activity. If we stay optimistic it extends telomere length, which enhances health and extends life.

Extending the length of telomeres by the activity of enzymes, called telomerases, could increase vitality and productivity of stem cells. Enhanced telomerase activity is the 'Fountain of Youth', and promotes a long and healthy life. Different life experiences or events happening in life can stimulate or suppress telomerase activity.

Stressful parental development, child abuse, domestic violence, post-traumatic stress disorder, nutritional deficiencies, and lack of love, all inhibit telomerase activity.

On the other hand, exercise, good nutrition, a positive outlook in life, living in happiness and gratitude, experiencing love and affection; all these factors enhance telomerase activity and promote a long and healthy life.

In a recent study it was found that breast cancer patients who were involved in mindfulness meditation, tended to preserve telomere length, whilst in a telomere control group, those without these interventions resulted in shorter telomere length; research on the telomere shows that 2% of the genome that encodes protein has a big impact on health and disease.

In an experiment done on cultured cells, it was found that approximately 50 generations of cells are produced before their telomeres are lost; then DNA replication produces defective protein, which causes the cell's death and compromises its ability to further divide

Humans have a finite life-span, determined by how many times stem cells divide and replace the billions of cells that die every day.

Elaine Fox, in her book "Sunny Brain and Rainy Brain", explains that there is a strong relationship between our genetic makeup and the environment in which we live. It means that our switching on or switching off, or down-regulation, or up-regulation of our genes are dependent on the environmental signals that they 'dial up' or switch up.

It means that our genes do not operate in isolation, but start signalling when interacting with the environment. So genes and the environment *can* work interdependently to develop our personality and outlook. The technologies of modern molecular genetics, neuroscience, and psychology have been much synergized to understand this mechanism. Consequently, if we develop a tendency to retrain our brains, we can alter our genetic code by positive thoughts.

The following are the main examples and evidences of expression of genes dependent on the kind of environment. Genes are a specific sequence of DNA, and as information in DNA is stored in the form of DNA codes, these codes are made up of four chemical bases which are called nucleotides; linked together as:

A=T (Adenine=Thymine)
G≡C (Guanine≡Cytosine)

When one base joins ribose sugar, and one phosphate molecule, they are called nucleotides. These four above nucleotides are core structures of DNA. The gene is the particular sequence of these nucleotide pairs. As DNA inherits from generation after generation, the sequence of DNA remains constant. When genes have variations in their structure they produce abnormal effects – mutations – in the body and brain. Gene mutations can have positive or negative effects.

These variations in genes are known as Single Nucleotide Polymorphism (SNP). These variations can develop into a disease or any specific personality trait. For example, the serotonin transporter gene and dopamine receptor gene affects the serotonin and dopamine level in the brain.

These two SNP changes in genes affect the mental states of the patient. The way by which these particular neurotransmitter systems affect the specific gene is known as *candidate gene approach*. The person carrying vulnerability genes has a particular SNP gene.

People carrying a vulnerability gene of lung cancer have a higher risk of developing lung cancer when they are exposed to carcinogenic compounds in food or through smoking.

Similarly, a vulnerability gene of anxiety will develop anxiety when susceptible people are exposed to stress and trauma.

COMT gene (catechol-O-methyltransferase):

A research study performed on the COMT gene by Danny Weinberger shows that the COMT gene is involved in production of dopamine balance in the brain; as dopamine maintains the pleasure system active in the brain, so too much dopamine causes schizophrenia.

Research studies show that insufficient COMT gene has poor activity in the prefrontal cortex of the brain, so variation in the COMT gene can be the cause of schizophrenia.

MAOA gene (monoamine oxidase A):

In another scientific study on the effect of the gene and environment in personality traits it was shown that:

Abused children with the low expression of MAOA gene develop serious mental health problems, and have been involved in criminal and antisocial behaviour, but children having the high expression of MAOA gene did not develop any serious mental health problems, even though they had serious abuse.

Epigenetics modifications are stable and passed on to future generations. They are changed in response to environmental stimuli. Epigenetics has influenced all aspects of biology; and has developed into one of the most important fields in biological science.

David Hamilton (2009) explained that genes can be activated by the state of mind. If you have a happier and positive state of mind, new genes will start signalling, and new beneficial proteins will be produced for mind and body.

But if you have pessimistic and toxic thoughts, the genes will signal the toxic proteins to the brain and body. Hence by changing our mind we can change our body at subatomic and cellular level.

As when a gene is switched on a new protein is produced, this protein may be involved in the construction of new cells and tissues, new bone cells, blood cells, or may be used to form immune systems.

This protein produced by activation of genes can be an enzyme that can catalyze other chemical reactions in formulations of new proteins and molecules.

For example – pepsin, an enzyme produced in the stomach, can convert food into digestive substances.

This protein produced by gene activation may be hormones, whose function is to message signalling to other cells.

Activations of genes by signals of our mind can produce hormones, such as growth hormones that help in healing wounds and other damaged tissues. It is found that mental and emotional stress reduces the level of growth hormone at wound sites.

It is found that due to stress, over one hundred genes are *down-regulated.* Similarly over 70 genes are *up-regulated* by cultivating pleasure and optimism, and by maintaining a gratitude attitude. So when over 70 genes are down-regulated it diminishes the healing of wounds by lack of growth hormones.

Consequently cultivating a feel-good and optimistic attitude increases the up-regulation of growth hormones at wound sites, as our thoughts affect our genes that are signalling for proteins. Mixtures of genes are involved in different functions.

If we have a family history of an oncogene (cancer-causing), or a cardiac failure gene, and if we keep worrying about the presence of them in our makeup, the risk is more likely that we will be the victim of cancer or heart disease.

But even if we have those genes in our genetic makeup, but we never concern ourselves about them, and keep ourselves in good dietary, environmental, and positive psychological conditions, then there are few chances of activation of these genes and we would be safe from this genetic risk; our 'instruction' can turn down the bad genes – "Sometimes ignorance is a blessing".

On the other hand our thoughts also influence the growth of stem cells because stem cells also have DNA that is controlled by environmental signals.

When the genes are activated, stem cells can become bone cells, immune cells, skin cells, heart cells, or blood cells, or can become neurons – stress though, can interfere with neurogenesis.

Embryonic stem cells can be transplanted into the liver or heart which can re-grow the damaged part of the organs. When a skin wound heals, stem cells travel from bone marrow into skin cells. Stem cells can also travel to bone marrow and into the heart cells and can regenerate damaged heart muscle.

CHAPTER 7

Neuroplasticity: Rewire and Alter the Structure of your Brain

The brain is not 'hard-wired'

According to Norman Doidge in his book, "The Brain That Changes itself":

Neuro means neuron or nerve cells in our brain or nervous system. Plastic means changeable, malleable, or modifiable. It means "that we see with our brain, not with our eyes". Neuroplasticity has implications for our understanding of how relationships, love, sex, greed, addiction, culture, technology, learning, and psychotherapies change our brain.

Neuroplasticity is the power of the mind that is capable of changing and expanding, and keeps on enhancing, with a positive interaction with the environment. Even a brain that has sustained injuries has the ability to rebuild itself by positive affirmation and by thinking about a certain goal, and can rewire the whole brain.

Now we know that we are not at the mercy of the genetically predetermined brain make-up, we can alter our brain structure and function by our positive and optimistic thinking.

Dr. Schwartz in his research studies proved by brain scanning that many OCD patients, stroke victims, and musicians have changed their brain for the better by applying the principles of *self-directed* neuroplasticity.

Previously it was thought that the brain was fixed and hard-wired, and that the teen years and mid-20's were the final stages of brain development.

Now, new research in the field of neuroscience shows that the brain is malleable, and is plastic in nature. If it could be rewired according to our behaviour towards our environment and instincts, then we can adapt and make new adaptive changes in our brain by adjusting ourselves in better environments and social situations. By learning new skills we make new connections in our memories, and we are keeping it changing in our whole life by learning new skills, languages, and new ways of doing things. By learning new skills we make new memory connections in our minds, and continue this process throughout our whole life by learning new skills, languages, and by new ways of doing things.

On the other hand foods such as blueberries, green tea, dark chocolate, vegetables, fish, fruits and nuts, enhances the building up of new neural connections in the brain, making it flourish.

In some neurodegenerative diseases and brain damage injuries the brain is able to respond to music therapies, brain wave entrainment therapies, meditation, and by mindfulness practises. By setting up achievable goals and aims in our lives, we could boost the plasticity of the brain and completely change its structure and functioning.

In a comparative research study reported by Elaine Fox in her book "Sunny Brain and Rainy Brain", London's black cab taxi drivers' fMRI scans showed that the back part of their brain, the hippocampus, was larger than that of the general population. This part of the brain is associated with navigation in birds, animals, and humans. As taxi drivers have to learn over 25,000 different streets in London to pass their taxi-driving test (The Knowledge), that is why the size of their hippocampus becomes bigger with spending more time in the taxi profession.

Professional Musicians and Neuroplasticity of their brain

Studies utilizing high resolution MRI brain scans of professional musicians show that the brains of musicians and non-musicians differ in significant ways. Music performance is regarded as one of the most impressive of all human achievements.

Studies on MRI-scanned brains of musicians and non-musicians show that the brain areas, which were involved in hearing complex sounds, are much larger in musicians than non-musicians. Research shows that music practise increases their relevant brain regions.

With the discovery of neuroplasticity, we can now understand that the brain is capable of more flexibility, and we have rejected the old notion that the brain is fixed and hard-wired. We now know that our brain never ceases to respond to new skills and our environmental stimulus; it is learning from birth and continues until we die.

Neuroscience research shows that a complex network of neurons and pathways of nerve fibres inside our head are constantly responding, adapting, and rearranging themselves. This flexibility presents us with great opportunities to change our outlook.

Plasticity of the brain increases when we challenge our brain with new things, beliefs, and ways of doing things differently. If we do not use parts of our brain, these brain areas will gradually be taken over by other functions, but if we make efforts, even deeply embedded circuits have the potential to change.

As in the past there have been evidences for neuroplasticity, so this science will make it possible in the future for new treatments for the range of degenerative brain disorders like Parkinson's, Alzheimer's and other neurological conditions.

It is speculated that mental health problems such as anxiety and depression may also be cured by this power of neuroplasticity.

Dr. David Hamilton, in "How your Mind Can Heal Your Body", reported a number of different successful experiments on different groups of patients, and the population generally, found that our five senses and 'sixth sense' perception, and conceiving stimulus in our mind, increases our brain plasticity.

When we perceive a new idea in our mind and start nurturing it in our brain, it causes millions of neurons, or brain cells, to fire, and wire together, which enhances the capacity of our mind to increase.

Meditation increases the thickness of the pre-frontal cortex in the brain. Visualizing good health, wealth, wellness, happiness, prosperity, and wisdom alter the microscopic structure of our brain and starts signalling new genes for beneficial proteins; so we can experience changes in our genetic makeup at subatomic level.

These new neural connections start dissolving stress, trauma, and start regenerating the damaged part of the brain that is injured. This is called the neurogenesis, or rewiring, of our brain by positive thinking. By surrendering our ego and prestige, replacing the emotions of hate, envy, judgement and competitive emotions with creative constructive criticism and curiosity, and by maintaining our joint struggle to conquer the mysteries of the universe, our brain plasticity will expand.

Neuroscience research shows that our brain has the capacity of neurogenesis to all areas of our brain.

As mentioned earlier, some antioxidant foods like blueberries, dark chocolate, green tea, and other nutrients available at herbal and synthetic drug stores, boost mental capacity and plasticity. The following amino acid supplements have powerful effects on repairing the brain atrophy caused by stress and have amazing effects to enhance brain plasticity

These amino acids have powerful effects on repairing the brain atrophy caused by stress and have amazing effects to enhance brain plasticity:

- **Ginkgo biloba:** Increases brain oxygen uptake. Helps neural growth.
- **L. Arginine:** Lowers blood pressure. Assists with increasing low libido.
- **Glycine:** Helps optimize sugar levels and sleep.
- **Acetylcholine (ACh):** A neuromodulator that can help repair brain atrophy and control motivation, arousal, and attention.
- **DL - phenylalanine:** Helps to treat chronic pain depression, attention deficit hyperactivity disorder (ADHD), Parkinson's disease, alcohol withdrawal symptoms, and a skin disease called vitiligo.
- **GABA:** Improves mood, relieves anxiety, improves sleep, and treats ADHD.

- **L-glutathione:** Treating alcoholism, weakened immune systems, memory loss, Alzheimer's and Parkinson's disease.
- **Ginseng:** Helps in cognitive functioning.

Power of your faith can cure and dissolve illness

David Hamilton explained the power of faith has a placebo effect in dissolving illness.

If we have strong faith and believe that our subconscious mind has all capabilities to bring out all the solutions of our spiritual and professional problems, then we can also apply this power of belief and faith in curing of illnesses.

For example, if we believe in certain drugs that will cure our illnesses even though that drug has not even the chemical substances for that disease, our faith in drugs makes our mind produce that active chemical in our brain that will really dissolve-out that kind of illness.

It has been proven by testing on some patients that merely by strengthening their belief and faith in drugs to cure illness will produce healing compounds from the brain that could actually cure the illness, even if they are given placebo drugs. Our mind itself is a big 'pharmacy' of many healing compounds/drugs, that even pharmaceutical companies have not yet made. Such drugs that a mind may produce just by strengthening faith on remedy for illness means that the placebo effects of the drugs are governed by the brain.

The brain itself can produce any type of compound, from painkillers to antidepressants; even spiritual healing methods have strong placebo effects on our mind and body.

Visualization and Affirmation

David Hamilton, in his book "How your mind can heal your body", describes many experimental evidences of the effects of visualization and affirmation that help to boost plasticity of mind and healing.

If you focus on a specific part of the body that is connected to the brain, as nerves connect the brain to the skin, muscles, bones, tendons and internal organs; for example, if we imagine moving our fingers, toes, or tongue, the area of the brain that governs these parts of the body is activated. As the nerves connect the brain to the muscles, that muscle also gets stronger, when we merely *imagine* using them.

Scientists tested the volunteers for different experiments, and they found that individuals who were doing real exercise of different parts of the body, contrasted with those who were only imagining that exercise, it was found that those who were just doing the imaginary exercise developed strength in those parts of the body.

The athletic community has long known that muscles can be affected by brain visualization strategies. Research has proven that the brain is stimulated by visualization which in turn stimulates optimal muscle performance. If an athlete regularly visualizes running for a world record at the required speed, it is likely that muscles will develop and perform differently than for those who did not use visualizing techniques. It is found that even just watching someone exercise can affect our brain and muscles.

In a research experiment performed on volunteers, they were only allowed to watch people moving their hands, mouth, and feet. By scanning the volunteer's brains it was found that areas that control hands, mouth and feet movements appeared to be activated and subsequently became more developed. If we watch an image while performing a particular skill and our brain muscles and body are stimulated, like an expert; it is generally tested in the neuroscience field that if someone is sad and you are paying attention to them, your brain will mirror the sadness on their face. If you spend enough time with a sad person, then the chances are that you will become sad too.

Similarly, if you spend time with happy people your brain will mirror their expression and action and your mood is likely to improve.

Mirror Neurons and Visualization

David Hamilton explained that research studies on the mimic ability of mirror neurons shows that when we hear a person speaking our tongue muscles are also activated; but the speaker in front of you should have a clarity in accent and voice.

Similarly, if you have impaired movement and someone is describing that movement with clarity of voice and tone, you will notice that your ability to move would increase and your brain map for that muscle would expand and you will soon notice that with increased brain map the area of your brain for those muscles will be expanded, and you will start moving your muscle.

On the other hand, for wellness and wellbeing aspects of neuroplasticity, if we are sick and if we just listen to someone who talks about perfect health, then our mind will automatically start healing itself for wellness. But in our society if we become sick, people start saying how sick we are; reinforcing the sick mentality and inhibiting the brain's wellness response.

Mirror neuron activity increases if we simply *look* at someone's body parts. This in consequence increases the sensitivity of our own body parts. Alternatively, if we only *visualize* another person's body parts, then our own body parts become 'mirrored', and sensitized; the brain does not know the difference between real scenes we observe and imaginary scenes that we visualize.

If we *visualize* good health and optimistic thoughts then appropriate chemicals are released and the right genes are activated or deactivated. Ultimately, we become what we are imagining, so it is good to listen to someone, or via audio/video, to get the benefit of positive imagining, to begin the healing processes in our mind. By instructed or guided imagery we may heal any ache, pain, or disease by looking, seeing, hearing and/or imagining.

Brain and body connections

As our brain is connected through our autonomic nervous system with eyes, lung, liver, spleen, stomach, pancreas, intestines, kidney, bladder, skin, and reproductive organs, our subconscious mind maintains all these systems unconsciously. That is why our belief, either conscious or subconscious, influences systems and organs of the body.

When we expect something to happen, that happens at both the peripheral and autonomic nervous systems, subsequently it can be concluded that our thoughts can change the structure and function of our brain.

These thoughts send chemicals from the brain throughout our body. These chemical systems then interact with cells, and even our genetic code. Research shows that if we focus on a part of our body, then the area of the brain that governs that part becomes activated, and that body part is also activated.

Affirmation

Affirmation means saying something repeatedly about our healing, wealth or happiness, because repetition will create neural connections in our brain. It generates more energy and neural connections become stronger. Then the mind triggers its journey to achieve that task. With repeatedly doing the following affirmations we are able to improve our health, relationships, knowledge, and wisdom. It is better to write down the affirmations and keep them in front of your mirror or study table, or verbally say them to yourself 20 times in the morning and before retiring to bed, so that with repeated exposure your brain can begin to transform itself.

How to safeguard your plastic mind from negative attitudes in society:

David Schwartz in his book 'Magic of Thinking Big' suggests the following strategies to protect our minds from negativity. As we are the product of our environment, so the association with negative people tends to make us think negatively; close contact with petty individuals develops petty habits in us.

Companionship and association with people with big ideas raises the level of our thinking. Close contact with ambitious people gives us ambition; your personality, ambitions, present status in life, is largely the result of your psychological environment.

The person you will be next year, in 5 years, ten years, or twenty, will depend on your future environment. You change over months and years, but how you will change depends upon your chosen environment.

Be persistent to achieve your goals

Successful people never surrender to suppressive forces. People who never surrender are the happiest because they accomplish most. They find life stimulating and rewarding. Each day they actively encounter with other successful people, creating new opportunities via new ideas and new circumstances.

They make new friends, join new organizations, and enlarge their social orbit; variety in people and things adds pleasure in life and gives it broader dimension. They also select friends who have views different from themselves. Responsibilities and positions of high status precipitate to persons who are able to see both sides.

In the challenges of the 21st century narrow individuals haven't much of a future.

"Favour of your subconscious mind"

When training your subconscious mind by affirmations and auto suggestions this task and goal is achievable. You set the timeline for that goal. Your subconscious mind promptly starts working on that goal and will bring to you hundreds of different solutions to achieve that goal.

Conversely, if you think about the goal and you consciously instigate negative auto-suggestions to your mind, such as, "I can't achieve this goal", then you may cause brain-procrastination. If you think and talk about that goal negatively, then your subconscious mind presents hundreds of reasons why this goal could not be achieved – *"As you sow, so shall you reap"*.

Chapter 8

Music Therapies: Improve Neurodegenerative Diseases.

Alzheimer's, Parkinson's, and Autism

Monique Van Bruggen-Rufi, in her research paper, defines and explains the history and role of music in neurodegenerative diseases as:

"Music Therapy is the clinical and evidence-based interventions to accomplish certain goals within a therapeutic relationship by professional music therapists."

She explained that, "music therapies assess emotional wellbeing, physical health, social functioning, communication abilities, and cognitive skills through musical responses".

Oliver Sacks, in his book, "Musicophilia", explained that "listening to music is not just auditory and emotional, it is also a motoric activity – we listen to music with our muscles."

"Our faces and postures mirror the 'narrative' of the melody, and the thoughts and feelings it provokes".

Research on the effect of music on different neurological conditions is a new field of neurology. As music activates various regions of the brain, music can assist recovery in brain injuries and neurodegenerative diseases.

Listening to music can alter brain structure and function, but the molecular mechanism behind these phenomena is still unknown.

A research study in Finland, by Chakravarthi Kanduri et al, 2015, has reported that "music listening can cause physiological changes in cerebral blood flow, cardiovascular muscle functioning, and can also enhance dopamine secretion in the brain".

Music listening can regulate emotions and feelings of pleasure. Music is now being used as a therapeutic tool in clinical settings.

A systematic literature review published by Monique Van Bruggen-Rufi in 2015 in the Netherlands, reported that, "….if we perform MRI to visualize the brain of music listeners, we will find that there are involvements in broad networks of the brain regions. Music listening can trigger the brain network in pre-frontal and interior frontal cortex, superior temporal poles and the cerebellum".

And it was found that "if the music is emotionally meaningful to the listener, it activates the ventral tegmental area, the accumbens nucleus, and the hypothalamus".

It has been reported in this study that "there is a special relationship between music and motor neural circuits. It means that music can improve the movement problems of patients with Parkinson's disease and Huntington's disease". Music could activate the neural pathways in the brain regions like the insula, cingulate, cortex, hypothalamus, hippocampus, amygdala, and pre-frontal cortex. These regions could be activated by music and can provoke certain responses in these areas of the brain.

This research study performed by Monique Van Bruggen-Rufi suggests that patients with dementia, age-related conditions, developmental learning disabilities, addictions, brain injuries, physical disabilities, or acute/chronic pain, could benefit from this treatment.

Motor, cognitive, psychiatric, emotional, and social disturbances can be targeted by Music Therapies.

Music Therapy can treat symptoms of neurological diseases

Lauren Banker defines Alzheimer's disease as "gradual neurodegenerative disease in which there is a formation of plaque growth, neuron decay, and formation of neuro-fibrillary tangles throughout the brain, which causes cognitive behavioural and emotional deterioration, such as memory and language impairment".

Music therapy is one of the most cost-effective alternative therapies for Alzheimer's disease; in which music is used to treat cognitive, behavioural, and emotional symptoms. Music therapy is performed in two ways.

(a) Interactive or active.
(b) Passive or receptive.

Interactive or active therapy patients sing, hum, move along with music, or play an instrument, whereas passive or receptive therapy patients only listen to live or recorded music, and are less involved.

The following symptoms of Alzheimer's disease are improved by music therapy

1. Improved memory:

Music therapy greatly improves recall of old memories. When patients sing a familiar song it enhances recall of their date of birth and past memories. It also helps to form new memories. It means that music therapy acts as a catalyst to remembering old memories and forming new ones.

2. Improved language functioning and communication:

Music therapy also improves language functioning and communications. Impaired language functioning is caused by Alzheimer's disease. Patients with this disease cannot comprehend and produce language and have impaired judgement and experience difficulty in expressing themselves.

When patients sing in therapy sessions they become able to comprehend the topics of conversation better and stay on topic more frequently.

They have increased communication and interaction with others, become socially more interactive, show improved greeting and complimenting behaviours, and begin sharing jokes and memories.

3. Improved behavioural symptoms:

Alzheimer's sufferers become more agitated when they experience difficulty in articulating their thoughts, needs, or desires – music therapy helps to reduce the agitated behaviours, including aimless wandering, verbal and physical aggression, repetitive sentences or questions, and complaining. Patients who have been engaged in music therapy by *singing*, and *playing* instruments, exhibit reduced agitated behaviours.

Those who *listen* to music exhibit less agitated behaviours, become less insulting, are less attention-seeking, complaining, and show reduction in psychotic and psychological symptoms.

4. Improved psychological functioning:

Music therapy also improves psychological symptoms of Alzheimer's patients who have been exposed to *extended* therapy. It reduces symptoms of paranoia, hallucination, and anxiety.

5. Improved emotional symptoms:

Music therapy has been effective in improving emotional symptoms of Alzheimer's patients. Therapy reduces negative effects, such as stress. It also helps to elevate positive emotions and improve patient's mood.

After extensive music therapy patients feel more positive, and they have an increased sense of belonging and accomplishment.

Parkinson's disease and music therapy

In Parkinson's disease most patients suffer from abnormality of voice and speech. Traditional pharmacological treatments and other speech therapies have not been particularly effective in treating these abnormalities. Consequently 80% of Parkinson's sufferers have difficulty speaking intelligibly, severely impairing their communication skills, and their ability to convey their emotional states and needs.

A comparative study by Catherine Y. Wan, et al, in Harvard Medical School, reported that "an intensive voice therapy programme can be effective in minimizing some of the speech abnormalities in patients with Parkinson's disease".

It is reported in the research studies that these improvements in speech abnormalities could be maintained even after 12 months of termination of treatment.

A research study by Bennedetto et al, 2008, shows that there is a significant improvement in vowel phonation and reading of the patients after 13 sessions of choral singing, which shows that singing could help to improve speech-related complications and disorders in Parkinson's patients.

Music Therapy and Autism

Autism is a condition in which there is impairment in expression of language and communication. This condition affects about 1% of the population. Some autistic individuals have an almost total lack of functional speech.

Music therapy is helpful in improving this condition. Music intervention, designed to treat children with autism, is known as Auditory Motor Mapping Training (AMMT). This intervention involves three main components – singing, motor activity, and imitation.

This therapy engages the dysfunctional human mirror neuron system that is believed to be impaired in Autism.

AMMT enhances interaction between the auditory and motor systems, which is considered to be an effective therapy through which individuals with autism can develop their communication skills.

In Autism the Impaired Language System is lateralized to the left hemisphere. Singing or intoned speaking engages a larger bi-hemispheric network. So when the words are sung, the phonemes are isolated, which are helpful in self-correction. Singing may help to engage a brain network that facilitates sound motor mapping.

Music therapy alters human transcriptome

Chakravarthi Kanduri, et al 2015, studied the effect of listening to music on human transcriptome, reporting some significant changes in transcriptome of those who had actively participated in music therapy sessions.

Music has been an important part of cultural rituals in most societies. Nowadays neurophysiological studies show that listening to, or performing, music has lasting effects on human brain structure and function. Listening to classical and soothing music has a profound effect on body and brain. It regulates blood flow, improves heart and muscle functions, and increases dopamine secretion in the human brain. Music evokes pleasure and regulates human emotions.

Other practical applications of music therapy

Arthur R. Pell, in his revised edition of Napoleon Hill's "Think and grow rich", explained the effect of music therapy applied to his young child born without any external or internal ear mechanisms. Pell explained that by applying music therapy, supported by his own *modus operandi* of faith and desire; he successfully recovered the hearing of his deaf and mute child. The child appeared to respond to the music therapy, and later Pell decided the child needed further support and was instrumental in developing a suitable hearing aid, in partnership with hearing aid companies.

He then did a lot of research and rendered his services to hearing aid instrument manufacturing companies for deaf and mute people.

Ancient Mystics used Music therapy to heal

The ancient mystics were aware of the healing effects of music on body and mind. They used music therapy to heal many emotional disturbances. In modern times we have music therapy, mantras, and tuning forks to help to adjust our behavioural and emotional issues.

Quantum physicists and mystics believe that "everything in the universe is made up of vibration frequencies".

CHAPTER 9

Meditation & Mindfulness: Combat Neurodegenerative Diseases

<u>*"Trained Minds are psychologically different from Untrained Minds"*</u>

Meditation is a 'magical' drug for most mental and physical health conditions. Meditation can open your heart and mind for wellbeing of yourself and those around you. Meditation practising concepts were brought to Western societies in the twenty-first century by Eastern peoples and communities.

If you regularly practise meditation it will bring profound positive effects in your mind, body, and soul. Meditation practise, if you do it properly and regularly, will bring a chain of positive chemical reactions in your body; it will bring an inner balance in your life by strengthening the intuition.

Meditation will connect your inner and outer universal divine energy and bring balance and harmony with you and other people. Your self-esteem will go high; your attitude and vision toward life and people will change.

By practising meditation you transform from your past damaging and toxic thoughts, to constructive future relationships and achievements.

By encompassing these health and well-being qualities, meditation has been considered a therapeutic practise. It will set new goals, aims, and direction in your future life.

Meditation brings a great impact on the human brain – its end results and benefits can be harnessed, and by properly practising it you can enjoy the fruits of creativity, compassion, generosity, bliss, and joy in life.

Functional magnetic resonance imaging (fMRI) of results from trained and untrained meditated minds shows profound differences in their structure and anatomy.

Naomi Ozaniec in her book "Beat Stress with Meditation" claims that "a correlation between mental activity and brainwave patterns has been known since the 1960's"; her findings have fuelled a cultural revolution that is centred on spiritualization of values by introducing meditation principles of visualization, relaxation, and mindfulness techniques; according to Ozaniec, bio-feedback has moved to neuro-feedback.

Western objective empiricism technology and Eastern subjective experience technology has now opened up the new era of Mind-Brain Interface Technology.

The big questions of Western science and philosophy is whether 'mind' is created by the brain, and whether consciousness itself might be reduced to neural activity. To answer these questions Buddhism proposes a model that places mind beyond brain.

Meditation practises are regarded as beneficial to alter the structure and anatomy of the brain. Although meditation is a passive process, when it involves loving, kindness, and compassion practises, it brings both short-term and long-term neural changes.

Nowadays, by the application of (fMRI), where Buddhist meditation meets Western technology, makes advancement in brain research – so it is found, that the brain has the capacity to develop new neural connections throughout life, which means that this neuroplasticity of the brain can make it possible to recover from injury and disease.

In a recent research report from the 'New York Academy of Sciences', Daniel A. Monti writes, "Meditation Techniques present a potential adjuvant treatment for patients with neurodegenerative diseases and are regarded as inexpensive and easy to teach and perform".

Meditation helps to improve cognition and memory in patients with neurodegenerative diseases. This review by Daniel A. Monti discusses the current data on meditation, memory, and attention. It also describes the potential application of meditation in patients with neurodegenerative disease.

Research by Rafal Marciniak et al, in "Frontiers in Behavioural Neuro-science" (2014), reported that a large number of people suffer from dementia, Alzheimer's, and other neurodegenerative diseases, with aging. The researchers pointed out that in the future there will be a need for appropriate therapy for these patients; based on both pharmacological and non-pharmacological intervention. They concluded that Meditation Techniques are one of the best possibilities of non-pharmacological interventions, which is now a subject of great scientific interest.

There are different categories of meditation based on focus on single aspects, like breath or sounds. They are considered as concentration-meditation.

Another category of meditation is based on aspiring to gain open attention, which contains more objects at once, or are selected in consecutive order. This category is based in awareness, or open meditation. We can also divide meditation based on cognitive processes such as thought and images.

A third category is focused your general mental development and cultivating a state of wellbeing, or it may be based on mental qualities like love concentration, or wisdom.

A review published by Alison in 2015 reported that "meditation can change the size of key regions of our brain, improve our memory, and make us more empathetic, compassionate, and resilient under stress." According to this review different meditation practises are receiving growing attention.

fMRI studies in various experiments show that meditation can be a beneficial and suitable non-pharmacological intervention to combat cognitive decline in the elderly. Meditation-intervention improves the symptoms of Alzheimer's disease, and cognition in the elderly.

The other risk factors associated with Alzheimer's disease, such as hypertension, high cholesterol levels, poor cerebral blood flow, can be controlled by the impact of meditation on these patients.

An experiment reported by Rafal Marciniak et al, 2014, that when 73 to 83 year-old elderly patients were randomly divided into three groups; two based on different meditation techniques, and a control group without any intervention. Patients who were given transcendental meditation, and mindfulness meditation, performed twice a day for 20 minutes at periods of 12 weeks, were transformed.

Furthermore when the patients were examined and studied, the effect of meditation intervention improved cognitive flexibility, memory and verbal fluency, after 18 months and then after 36 months. The results suggest that the strong improvement was in patients who used transcendental meditation, followed by mindfulness meditation; and the worst results were in control groups and in those with only relaxation programmes.

Even testing after 3 years showed 100% effects in persons using transcendental meditation, and 87.5% effects were found in those with mindfulness meditation programmes.

Similarly, in another study to test the effect of Zen meditation on the decrease of grey matter thickness, it was found that the meditation increases the grey matter thickness in those who had Zen meditation intervention therapy.

fMRI scans of meditating elderly patients show structural changes in several regions, such as increased cortical thickness.

Most frequent changes reported are structural alterations in the anterior cingulate cortex superior and inferior frontal cortex pre frontal cortex. These regions are found to be involved in attention and perceiving internal sensory processes and cognitive functions. Some studies have reported increased volume of the hippocampus which is important for memory.

Meditation is the 'Fountain of Youth'.

Meditation increases brain grey matter and optimizes brain functioning – those who meditate purposefully can achieve a new state of consciousness and become successful in improving both their mental and physical health. Skilful and productive meditation requires conscious practise effort.

Meditation can improve concentration and intelligence, and lessens anxiety and depression. You can experiment with the different meditation methods available to choose the most appropriate for you.

- *'Concentration-based Meditation'* will improve your concentration.

- *'Mindful Meditation'* will improve your mood.

Meditation can be practised several times daily, once a day, weekly, or even monthly. However, most experts recommend you meditate every day for 10 - 30 minutes to get the full benefit; whichever you feel most comfortable with.

Incorporating meditation into your life is recommended for re-balancing our bodies.

Chemistry of the Meditating Brain:

Serotonin: meditation boosts serotonin, which is a mood-controlling neurotransmitter.

Cortisol: meditation neutralizes cortisol, which is a major age-accelerating hormone. In stress our body produces a lot of cortisol and adrenaline, which leads to anxiety, depression, increased blood pressure, brain fog, insomnia, and inflammation. Mindfulness meditation reduces cortisol.

Dehydroepiandrosterone (DHEA): is a life-longevity molecule; the most important hormone in the body. As we get older our DHEA levels decrease year after year. Low levels make us more susceptible to disease, and accelerated aging. By measuring DHEA levels, we can estimate physiological 'true age'. The lower your DHEA level is, the fewer years you have left. But meditation provides a dramatic boost to DHEA hormone levels. Meditation practitioners have 43.7% more DHEA than anyone else.

Gamma-aminobutyric acid (GABA): makes you feel calm. Alcohol, drugs, tobacco, and caffeine addictions reduce the levels of GABA in the body. Lack of GABA can cause anxiety, nervousness, racing heart, and sleeplessness. It is found that levels of GABA increase by 27% after 60 minutes of mindfulness meditation.

Endorphin: meditation boosts endorphin levels. It is the hormone of happiness. It is produced in the body and used as an internal painkiller. After long-distance running endorphins rush in to the body, resulting in a heightened sense of wellbeing; that is why many runners are 'addicted' to their sport. The good news is that this wonderful state of mind can be achieved through meditation.

Growth Hormone (GH): meditation boosts growth hormone. High levels of GH are produced during childhood, sustained in the body until after entering your 40's, when growth hormone begins to decrease. Depletion of GH from the body causes weaker bones and muscles, poor heart contraction, bad moods, lack of motivation, fatigue, and increases body fat. Growth hormones are released during meditation, and the deepest state of sleep, called the *delta state*. That is why meditators generally look young and healthy.

Growth hormones are produced in our pituitary gland, which is situated at the base of the brain.

Melatonin: meditation boosts melatonin levels in the body. Produced by the pineal gland, its level in the blood increases throughout waking hours, and is at its peak just before going to sleep.

Meditation practitioners have 98% increases in melatonin levels. Melatonin strengthens the immune system, slows down aging, and prevents cancer. It may be involved in the prevention of over 100 different diseases; it is key to good mood and restful sleep.

Mindfulness can heal neurological diseases and disorders

Dr. Jessamy Hibberd and Jo Usmar, in their book "Make you Mindful", define mindfulness as "Mindfulness is a practise of awareness". It is a technique for learning to become more aware of your thoughts, emotions, body, impulses, urges, and the world around you. Mindfulness is a brilliant way of getting to know oneself better.

Mindfulness is not a quick fix. It is a skill that you have to learn like any other, e.g. cooking, playing games, drawing and skiing. Mindfulness requires time to learn and practise, and also energy. If you stick with it – you will get lots of reward.

After practising it, you will find yourself more engaged with life. You will find yourself more present in everything you do. If you have thoughts and doubts in mind about your future, and unresolved past issues, mindfulness will make your life happier, exciting, and wonderful – you will become able to deal with upsetting or stressful things.

Marchand, W. R. (2011) reported in "World Journal of Radiology" that "Mindfulness practise is the moment-by-moment awareness of sensations, emotions, and thoughts".

"Mindfulness-based interventions are used for stress, psychological wellbeing, coping with chronic illness, and are used as adjunctive treatments for psychiatric disorders; but the neural mechanism associated with mindfulness has not yet been well characterized"

fMRI studies show that mindfulness impacts the function of the pre frontal medial cortex, insula, and amygdala. Mindfulness practise affects lateral frontal regions, basal ganglia, and the hippocampus.

A research study by Strauss, et al, (2014) describes that, "mindfulness-based interventions for anxiety and depression can reduce the risk of relapse for people with a history of depression". Zeidan. F, in 2014, reported the review literature from the 'Neuro-biology of Mindfulness' that mindful meditation can improve a range of mental and physical health problems. He has reported that neuro-imaging is beginning to identify the brain mechanisms that mediate the relationships between mindfulness, meditations, and the results obtained by such interventions. Mindfulness meditations can result in enhancement in sensory awareness, cognition; hence health and wellbeing can be accomplished through meditation practise.

Glossary

Abundance: a great, plentiful amount, an overflowing fullness, ample sufficiency, profusion, copious supply, superfluity of wealth – in the context of this book it is more than merely material wealth or possessions.

Accumbens: the nucleus accumbens (NAc) is a key brain region mediating a variety of behaviours, including reward and satisfaction, addiction, the regulation of emotions induced by music, and its connected role in mediating dopamine release. The NAc has a role in rhythmic timing and is considered to be of central importance to the limbic-motor interface.

Affluence: having a great amount of monetary wealth, land, and/or an unfettered beneficiary of scarce resources.

Amygdala: an almond-shaped mass of nuclei (cells) located deep within both temporal lobes of the brain. There are two amygdalae, one in each brain hemisphere. The amygdala is a limbic system structure involved in many of our emotions and motivations, particularly those related to survival; processing emotions such as fear, anger, and pleasure.

Articulated: able to express thoughts and feelings easily and clearly, or showing this quality.

Autism: is part of a range of conditions known as autistic spectrum disorders (ASD) that affect the way the brain processes information. Autism is a developmental disorder that can cause problems with social interaction, language skills and physical behaviour, and the world can appear chaotic with no clear boundaries, order or meaning. The disorder varies from mild, to so severe that sufferers may be almost unable to communicate and need round-the-clock care.

Basal ganglia: a group of nuclei (clusters of neurons) in the brain that is located deep beneath the cerebral cortex (the highly convoluted outer layer of the brain). Basal ganglia specialize in processing information on movement and in fine-tuning the activity of brain circuits that determine the best possible response in a given situation (e.g., using the hands to catch a ball or using the feet to run). Thus, they play an important role in planning actions that are required to achieve a particular goal, in executing well-practised habitual actions, and in learning new actions in novel situations.

Bliss: delight, ecstasy, euphoria, rapture, gladness, blessedness, joy, exaltation, satisfaction, pleasure, happiness, paradise – the opposite of distress, grief, woe, misery, anguish, unhappiness, heartbreak and wretchedness.

Cerebellum: the part of the brain located in the posterior cranial fossa behind the brainstem. It consists of two cerebellar lobes, and a middle section called the vermis. Three pairs of peduncles link it with the brainstem. Its functions are concerned with coordinating voluntary muscular activity.

Cerebral cortex: a thin mantle of grey matter covering the surface of each cerebral hemisphere. The cerebral cortex is crumpled and folded, forming numerous convolutions (gyri) and crevices (sulci). It is made up of six layers of nerve cells and the nerve pathways that connect them. The cerebral cortex is responsible for the processes of thought, perception and memory and serves as the seat of advanced motor function, social abilities, language, and problem solving.

Cingulate cortex: a component of the limbic system of the brain, responsible for producing emotional responses to physical sensations of pain.

Cognitive: relating to mental processes concerned with the knowing, perception, memory, judgment, and reasoning, as contrasted with emotional and volitional processes, etc.

COMT-Gene: provides instructions for making and maintain appropriate levels of the enzyme, catechol-O-methyltransferase. It is particularly important in the brain's prefrontal cortex, which is involved with personality, planning, inhibition of behaviours, abstract thinking, emotion, and working (short-term) memory, organizing and coordinating information from other parts of the brain.

Comprehended: understand the nature or meaning of; grasp with the mind; perceive.

Consciousness: a complex concept, one that includes memory, cognition, input from the senses, and an awareness of selfhood; essentially, the cognition of one's self, one's past, and one's potential futures, and the relationship between the mind and the physical world, at any given moment.

Creative Imaginative Faculty of Mind: is where the finite mind of Man has a direct communication with the *'Infinite Intelligence'* through the faculty of creative imagination, in which "hunches" and "inspirations" are claimed to be received. Creative imagination works only when the conscious mind is 'vibrating' rapidly, and stimulated through the emotion of strong desire. Great business leaders and artists, musicians, poets, and writers, become great because they developed the faculty of creative imagination.

Delta state (of sleep): one of 5 different wavelengths that function in the brain – alpha, beta, *delta*, gamma, and theta. In our deepest sleep state delta brain waves are dominant. Delta waves are the *slowest* recorded brain waves in human beings. They are found most often in infants and young children. As we age, we tend to produce fewer delta brain waves, even during deep sleep. Delta waves are associated with the deepest levels of relaxation and restorative, healing sleep. Adequate production of delta waves helps us feel rejuvenated after a good sleep. If there is abnormal delta activity, an individual may experience learning disabilities or have difficulties maintaining conscious awareness (such as in cases of brain injuries).

Dementia: not a disease in itself, but a progressive disorder; a group of symptoms that may accompany a number of diseases that affects the brain, particularly the ability to remember, think and reason. The most common of these is Alzheimer's disease. Another is vascular dementia which can develop following a stroke or if there is blood vessel damage that interrupts the flow of blood to the brain. Dementia is not a consequence of growing old but the risk of having dementia increases with age.

Dissuaded: to prevent someone from a purpose or course of action by persuasion.

Dopamine: a neurotransmitter produced by the brain, having several different functions, playing a critical role in the function of the central nervous system. It is also linked with the brain's complex system of motivation and reward. Altered levels of this neurotransmitter in the brain can cause a range of symptoms and problems, ranging from Parkinson's disease to Attention Deficit Disorder (ADD). In Parkinson's, low dopamine levels make patients shaky, weak, and confused, with impaired control over their bodies.

Eating disorders: are characterised by an abnormal attitude towards food that causes someone to change their eating habits and behaviour, leading them to make unhealthy choices about food with damaging results to their health. E.g. *anorexia nervosa* – when a person tries to keep their weight as low as possible by starving themselves and/or exercising excessively. *Bulimia* – when a person goes through periods of binge eating and then makes themselves deliberately vomit or uses laxatives to try to control their weight.

Endorphins: our natural pain and stress fighters, endorphins are among the brain chemicals known as neurotransmitters, which help transmit electrical signals within the nervous system. At least 20 types of endorphins have been demonstrated in humans. They interact with the opiate receptors in the brain to reduce our perception of pain and act similarly to drugs such as morphine and codeine.

Emotional intelligence: a description of how well an individual is able to be in touch with their feelings, and sense how those around them are feeling, to determine a best course of action when a choice must be made. It is not an inherent skill; anyone can learn, develop and apply it. Potentially dangerous situations can develop if people use their emotional intelligence in a way that benefits them only. By understanding the core emotions of those around us, and the negatives can be balanced properly, emotional intelligence will always be important.

Epigenetics: study of potentially heritable changes in gene expression (active versus inactive genes) that does not involve changes to the underlying DNA sequence – which in turn affects how cells read the genes. Epigenetic change is regular and natural but can also be influenced by factors including age, the environment/lifestyle. Research is continuously uncovering the role of epigenetics in a variety of human disorders and fatal diseases.

Expression of genes: gene expression is the process by which the genetic code – the nucleotide sequence – of a gene is used to direct protein synthesis and produce the structures of the cell. Thus gene expression involves two main stages:

Transcription – the production of messenger RNA (mRNA) by the enzyme RNA polymerase, and the processing of the resulting mRNA molecule.

Translation – the use of mRNA to direct protein synthesis, and the subsequent post-translational processing of the protein molecule.

Frontal cortex: consists of the two lobes at the front of the head, just behind the forehead, considered the hub of most of the higher brain functions, understanding, and most of our behavioural traits. Most long-term planning, emotional regulation, problem solving, impulse control, and motor skills functions are based in this area of the brain.

Genetic makeup: the genetic makeup of an organism is known as its genotype. The genotype refers to the set of traits found within the cells of living organisms. These traits, known as the genetic code, are passed from one generation to another during cell division and reproduction. "Genetic makeup" refers to the genes that determine what you look like and what physical characteristics you have; the colour of your eyes, your blood type, hair texture, or the structure of your digestive enzymes, etc.

Grey brain matter: contains most of the brain's neuronal cell bodies, and refers to unmyelinated neurons and other cells of the central nervous system. It is present in the brain, brainstem and cerebellum, and throughout the spinal cord. The grey matter includes regions of the brain involved in muscle control, and sensory perception such as seeing and hearing, memory, emotions, speech. For many years it was believed that the human brain is essentially hard-wired, that we are born with a set of cognitive abilities, such as the ability to learn language, which are more or less unalterable for the rest of our lives. But the discovery of neuroplasticity – our brain's ability to selectively transform itself – refers to our brain's *malleability*; its ability to respond to certain intrinsic or extrinsic stimuli by reorganizing its structure, function and connections.

Hippocampus: a brain region of the brain associated primarily with memory. The name hippocampus is derived from the Greek (*hippos*, meaning "horse," and *kampos*, meaning "sea monster"); since its structure resembles that of a sea horse. The hippocampus, which is located in the inner (medial) region of the temporal lobe, forms part of the limbic system, which is particularly important in regulating emotional responses. The hippocampus is principally thought to be involved in storing long-term memories and in making those memories resistant to forgetting, though this is a matter of debate. It is also thought to play an important role in spatial processing and navigation.

Hum: a sound made by producing a wordless tone with the mouth opened or closed, forcing the sound to usually emerge from the nose. Emit a prolonged droning sound like that of the speech sound often with a melody.

Hunches in the mind: are formed out of our *past experiences and knowledge.* Hunches, often referred to as *intuitions,* or *gut feelings,* don't always lead to good decisions, but are not nearly as flighty a concept as they may seem:

- "Trust your hunches. They're usually based on facts filed away just below the conscious level." – Dr. Joyce Brothers.
- "All human knowledge thus begins with intuitions, proceeds thence to concepts, and ends with ideas." – Immanuel Kant.
- "The intuitive mind is a sacred gift and the rational mind is a faithful servant. We have created a society that honours the servant and has forgotten the gift." – Albert Einstein.

Huntington's disease: a progressive disease of the nervous system marked by tremor, muscular rigidity, and slow, imprecise movement, chiefly affecting middle-aged and elderly people. It is associated with degeneration of the basal ganglia of the brain and a deficiency of the neurotransmitter dopamine.

Hypothalamus: its primary function is homeostasis, maintaining the body's status quo, system-wide. A section of the brain responsible for the production of many of the body's essential hormones, that govern physiological functions such as temperature regulation, thirst, hunger, sleep, mood, sex drive, and the release of other hormones within the body. This area of the brain houses the pituitary gland, and although this portion of the brain is small, it is involved in many necessary processes of the body including behavioural, autonomic (involuntary or unconscious), and endocrine functions, such as metabolism, growth and development.

Infinite intelligence: supposedly the glue that connects all living things with a "higher intelligence". It links the senses to the conscious mind and is the inspiration that seems to flow from another place. Whether you believe in God, or just in the existence of a 'higher intelligence', its adherents believe *"Infinite Intelligence"* is everywhere in the universe, and that it comes *from* it to us, and flows back *to* it from us, in a constant ebb and flow.

Insula: an oval region found in each hemisphere of the cerebral cortex, situated within the sylvian fissure, involved in sensation, emotion, and autonomic function.

Invigorated: an idea, a concept, philosophy, thing, or person, that makes you feel fresher, healthier, energetic, driven, focussed, or inspired.

Limbic brain: a system of the brain containing a group of structures that govern emotions and behaviour. The limbic system, and in particular the hippocampus and amygdala, is involved in the formation of long-term memory, and is closely associated with the olfactory structures (sense of smell).

MAOA gene: (monoamine oxidase A): Also known as the "warrior gene", involved in preparing the mind and body for action, the MAOA gene manifests as an aggressive trait which shows more with provocation. Monoamine oxidase A is an enzyme that breaks down important neurotransmitters in the brain, including dopamine, norepinephrine, and serotonin. Studies found a link between the low activity form of MAOA and heightened aggression. It cannot be prevented by diet, or medication, but is controllable, and you can refrain from "psychotic outbreaks".

Meditation: a mental practise where an individual trains the mind or induces a mode of consciousness, either to realise some benefit or for the mind to simply acknowledge its content without becoming identified with that content, or as an end in itself.

Mind empowerment: a multi-dimensional social and psychological training process that helps people gain personal development and control over their own lives and communities, by acting on issues that they define as important; the concept of empowerment depends upon the idea that power can 'expand our minds', e.g. NLP – the practise of understanding how people can filter and organise their mental maps of the world – thinking, feeling, language and behaviour – to provide a methodology to achieve outstanding performance.

Mindfulness: the psychological process of bringing one's attention to the internal and external experiences occurring in the *present moment*, which can be developed through the practise of meditation and other training. The popularity of mindfulness in the 'West' is generally considered to have been initiated by Jon Kabat-Zinn in the latter part of the 20th Century.

Mirror neuron: a neuron that fires both when an animal acts and when the animal observes the same action performed by another. Thus, the neuron "mirrors" the behaviour of the other, as though the observer were itself acting. In humans, brain activity consistent with that of mirror neurons has been found in the premotor cortex, the supplementary motor area, the primary somatosensory cortex and the inferior parietal cortex.

Motor neurons: first identified around 1898, they are nerve cells that conduct impulses to a muscle, gland, or other effector, making them either contract or relax. In humans, movement of the articulated internal skeletal structure is enabled by *coordinating* the contractions of the many muscles attached to it. Only the brain is capable of this complex coordination, and electrical signalling is arguably the only means fast enough to deliver its instructions to far flung muscles. The medium of delivery are electrically excitable cells called neurons.

Its basic structure includes a receptor on one end and a transmitter on the other, connected by an elongated body called the axon, some of which can be 39 inches (1m) long in humans. Chains of nerve cells, end to end, are bundled into nerve fibres which reach from the brain to the finger muscles and further.

Music therapy: a technique of complementary medicine that is an established psychological clinical intervention, which is delivered by professionally trained music therapists, to help people of all ages, whose lives have been affected by injury, illness or disability, through supporting their psychological, communicative, emotional, cognitive, physical, and social needs in a skilled manner.

Neurodegenerative diseases: include Parkinson's, Alzheimer's, and Huntington's. They occur as a result of incurable neurodegenerative processes, resulting in progressive degeneration and death. Research shows many similarities relate these diseases to one another on a sub-cellular level that offers hope for therapeutic advances that could ameliorate many diseases simultaneously.

Neurofibrillary tangles: intracellular clump of abnormal structures, composed of twisted masses of protein fibres within nerve cells made of insoluble protein, in the brain of patients with Alzheimer's disease.

Neuroplasticity: the brain's ability to reorganize itself by forming new neural connections throughout life. Neuroplasticity allows neurons (nerve cells) in the brain to compensate for injury and disease and to adjust their activities in response to new situations or to changes in their environment.

Neuroscience: a multidisciplinary branch of biology that studies the anatomy, biochemistry, molecular biology, physiology and development of neurons and neural circuits; focusing on the brain and its impact on behaviour and cognitive functions. Neuroscience is not only concerned with the normal functioning of the nervous system, but also what happens when people have neurodevelopmental, psychiatric, or neurological, disorders.

OCD (obsessive-compulsive disorder): in which a person commonly has obsessive thoughts and compulsive behaviours. Affecting men, women and children, this mental health condition can develop at any age. *Obsession* is an unwanted and unpleasant thought, image or urge that repeatedly enters the affected person's mind, causing feelings of anxiety, disgust or unease. *Compulsion* is a repetitive behaviour or mental act that the affected person feels they need to carry out to try to temporarily relieve the unpleasant feelings brought on by the obsessive thought.

Optimistic: positive psychology studies the positive impact that optimism has on mental and physical health. Optimists are sick less and live longer than pessimists. A positive outlook on life strengthens the immune system, and consequently the body's defences against illness and disease. Optimists have fewer heart attacks, tend to have enhanced responses in dealing with stress and mental illness, and they recover from illness faster.

Paranormal: Beyond the range of normal experience or scientific explanation.

Parapsychology: the scientific study of interactions between living organisms and their external environment that seems to transcend the known physical laws of nature, which is concerned with the investigation of paranormal and psychic phenomena.

Parkinson's disease: a progressive neurological condition affecting the brain. Symptoms are caused, in part, by reduced dopamine levels within the brain. Dopamine is a chemical used to transmit messages between brain cells. Brain cells within the region called the *basal ganglia* begin to deteriorate and levels of dopamine start to fall. When levels fall to about 60% of normal, movement symptoms begin to develop. It is not yet known why the cells start to deteriorate. Parkinson's causes both 'motor' and 'non-motor' symptoms.

<u>*Motor (or movement) symptoms consist of:*</u>

Tremor – involuntary shaking of arms, legs and/or head. It usually affects one side of the body before the other.

Rigidity – stiffness of the limbs.

Bradykinesia – slowness of movement; for example, difficulty turning over in bed or doing up buttons.

Postural instability – impaired postural reflexes; making it difficult to adjust or maintain balance.

<u>*Non-motor symptoms:*</u> can include depression, anxiety, pain, loss of sense of smell, sleep disturbance, bladder problems, constipation, and fatigue.

Pessimistic: pessimism is usually seen as is an entrenched negative habit of mind that can have disastrous consequences: depressed mood, resignation to negative experiences, underachievement and even poor physical and mental health. Although, some research seems to indicate that 'defensive pessimism' can result in positive outcomes.

Philanthropy: an altruistic concern for human advancement and welfare, usually manifested by donations of money, property, or work to needy persons, by endowment of institutions of learning and hospitals, and by generosity to other socially useful purposes.

Phoneme: the smallest meaningful unit of sound in a language. A meaningful sound is one that will change one word into another word. For example, the words cat and fat are two different words, but there is only one sound that is different between the two words – the first sound. That means that the "k" sound in cat and the "f" sound in fat are two different morphemes.

Shortly after birth, a baby begins to learn the phonemes of the language used around them. It is part of what they absorb as they learn language. We don't have to teach babies those sounds; their brains are 'hard-wired' to learn them as they interact with people. (It's one of the reasons it's good to talk to babies a lot.) As children continue to learn language they aren't consciously aware that words they are learning are made up of separate and very distinct sounds.

Placebo: a substance or other kind of 'treatment' that looks just like a regular treatment or medicine, but is not. It's actually an *inactive*, inert, treatment, injection, procedure, or substance. Typically, the person getting a placebo doesn't know the treatment isn't real, but the 'effect' can be real. The term "placebo effect" refers to the helpful effects a placebo has in relieving symptoms for a short time. It is thought to have something to do with the body's natural chemical ability to briefly relieve pain and certain other symptoms.

Prefrontal medial cortex (PFC): is located in the very front of the brain, just behind the forehead. In charge of abstract thinking and thought analysis, it is also responsible for regulating behaviour. This includes *mediating* conflicting thoughts, making choices between right and wrong, and predicting the probable outcomes of actions or events. This brain area also governs social control. The prefrontal cortex is the brain centre responsible for taking in data through the body's senses and deciding on actions; it is most strongly implicated in human qualities such as consciousness, general intelligence, and personality.

Quorum sensing: the regulation of gene expression in response to fluctuations in cell-population density. Quorum sensing bacteria produce and release chemical signal molecules called auto-inducers that increase in concentration as a function of cell density, which leads to an alteration in gene expressions that regulate a diverse array of physiological activities, including symbiosis, virulence, competence, conjugation, antibiotic production, motility, sporulation, and biofilm formation.

Single-nucleotide polymorphism: often abbreviated to SNP, is a variation in a single nucleotide that occurs at a specific position in the genome, where each variation is present to some appreciable degree within a population.

Synchronization: the coordination of events to operate a system in unison. The familiar conductor of an orchestra serves to keep the orchestra in time. Systems operating with all their parts in synchrony are said to be synchronous or in sync; those which are not are asynchronous.

Therapeutic: of or relating to the treating or curing of disease.

Tranquillity: the quality or state of peacefulness, calmness, quietude, or serenity.

Velopharyngeal: of or relating to the soft palate and the pharynx.

Ventral tegmental area: the origin of dopaminergic neurons of the mesolimbic and mesocortical systems, which project to the nucleus accumbens, amygdala, olfactory tubercle, and prefrontal cortex.

Visualizing: by visualizing a certain event, situation, or an object, you attract it into our life. It is a process similar to daydreaming. For some people, this might look like magic, but there is no magic involved, only the natural process of the power of thoughts and natural mental laws. It is like having a genie at your disposal.

Yoga: an ancient form of exercise focusing on postures to increase strength, flexibility, balance and enhanced breathing, to boost physical and mental wellbeing. There is evidence that regular yoga practise is beneficial for people with high blood pressure, heart disease, aches and pains depression and stress.

REFERENCES

1. Byrne, Rhonda, (2006), *The Secret,* UK: Simon and Schuster.
2. Chopra, Deepak, (2014), *You Can Transform Your Own Biology,* www.chopra.com/articles/you-can-transform-your-own-biology#sm.0000rb02nau2lebk1009ra1ze9c6n
3. Dispanza, Joe, (2014), *You are the Placebo,* UK: Hay House Inc.
4. Doidge, Norman, (2008), *The Brain that Changes Itself,* UK: Penguin Books.
5. Goleman, Daniel, (1998), *Working with Emotional Intelligence,* New York and Canada: Bantam Books.
6. Hamilton, David R, (2009), *How your Mind Can Heal your Body,* Hay House Inc.
7. Hibberd, Jessamy, & Usmar, Jo, (2015), *This Book will make you Mindful,* UK: Quercus Editions. Ltd.
8. Khera, Shiv, (2013), *You Can Win,* India: Bloomsbury.
9. Langley, Martha, (2015), *Mindfulness Made Easy,* UK: McGraw Hill.

10. Lipton, Bruce H, (2015), *The Biology of Belief,* UK: Hay House.
11. Ozeniec, Naomi, (2010), *Beat Stress with Meditation,* UK: McGraw Hill.
12. Pell, Arthur R, (2004), *Think and Grow Rich,* Vermilion/Edbury Publishing.
13. Schwartz, David, (2016), *The Magic of Thinking Big,* UK: Simon and Schuster.

Research papers reviewed

1. Banker, Lauren, (2015), *"The Effectiveness of Music Therapy in Treating Symptoms of Alzheimer's Disease"*. Department of Applied Psychology OPUS. http://steinhardt.nyu.edu/appsych/opus/issues/2015/fall/banker
2. Benioff Children's Hospital, UCSF, (2012), *"Treating Neurological Disorders with Music Therapy"*. https://www.ucsf.edu/news/2012/02/11600/treating-neurological-disorders-music-therapy
3. Kanduri, Chakravarthi, et al, (2015), *"The Effect of Listening to Music on Human Transcriptome"*. Peer J.3. https://peerj.com/articles/830/
4. Marchard, W.R. (2014), *"Neural Mechanism of Mindfulness and Meditation: Evidence from neuroimaging studies"*. World Journal of Radiology, 6: 471 – 479. https://www.ncbi.nlm.nih.gov/pmc/articles/PMC4109098/?report=classic
5. Marciniak, Rafal, et al, (2014), *"Effect of Meditation on Cognitive Functions in Context of Aging and Neurodegenerative diseases"*. Frontiers in Behavioural

Neuroscience 8:17. http://journal.frontiersin.org/article/10.3389/fnbeh.2014.00017/full
6. Masey, Alison, (2015), *"Mindfulness and Meditation effects on Cognition"*. Frontiers in behavioural neuroscience 8. https://www.worldcat.org/search?q=meditation+and+neurodegenerative+diseases&qt=owc_search
7. Monti, Daniel A. (2014), *"Meditation and neurodegenerative diseases"*. Annals of the New York Academy of Sciences ISSN0077-8923. https://www.worldcat.org/search?q=meditation+and+neurodegenerative+diseases&qt=owc_search
8. Van Bruggen-Rafi, Monique & Raymund Roos (2015), *"The Effect of Music Therapy for Patients with Huntington's disease"*. Journal of Literature and Art Studies, January 2015, Vol. 5, No. 1, 30-40 doi: 10.17265/21595836/2015.01.00 http://www.ziektevanhuntington.nl/upload/documenten/54febb5cb5a2e.pdf
9. Wan, Catherine Y, et al, (2010), *"The Therapeutic Effects of Singing in Neurological Disorders"*. 27(4): 287-295. https://www.ncbi.nlm.nih.gov/pmc/articles/PMC2996848/

Anees Akhtar
M.Phil. (Microbiology)
Lecturer, Tutor, and Mentor

Anees has an MSc in Botany, M.Phil. (Microbiology), (Pak). Post Graduate Diploma in Biotechnology, (UK).

He is working as a Neuroscience researcher and is a well-known scholar, thinker, motivational speaker, and seminar leader.

He has delivered many seminars and workshops in different universities and institutions in the UK and Pakistan.

His work in Neuroscience, Metaphysics, and Success-Philosophy is widely recognized and admired for its simplicity and clarity.

He possesses outstanding ability to transform minds from failure to success and from sickness to good health. His methods of teaching and grounding his philosophy are simple, effective, easily understood and implemented.

Muhammad Nasim Khan
PhD, PostDoc. USA.

Professor Dr Muhammad Nasim Khan has over 36 years of professional experience. He has been honorary visiting professor at St. Cloud State University (USA.).

He has been actively engaged in teaching and research activities at postgraduate, M.Sc., M.Phil. and Ph.D. level. A number of his research students have been awarded postgraduate degrees.

He has published numerous high impact factor research papers in peer reviewed international journals in the field of human molecular genetics, focusing on various human molecular genetic disorders, including neurodegenerative diseases.

In recognition of his marvellous research achievements Dr Khan has been adorned with three consecutive research productivity national awards by the PCST.

Nasim Khan has contributed his research expertise on neurodegenerative diseases in the development of this book.

Made in the USA
San Bernardino, CA
26 May 2018